Juvenile/Art

List of Materials:

- Pencils
- Eraser
- Ruler
- Scissors
- White Glue
- Poster Paints
- Paint Brushes
- Construction Paper
- Poster Board
- Tissue Paper

See detailed list pages 6, 7

Beginners Art Series

Age: 9 & Up

ISBN 0-929261-31-3

The Walter Foster
Instructional Art Book System

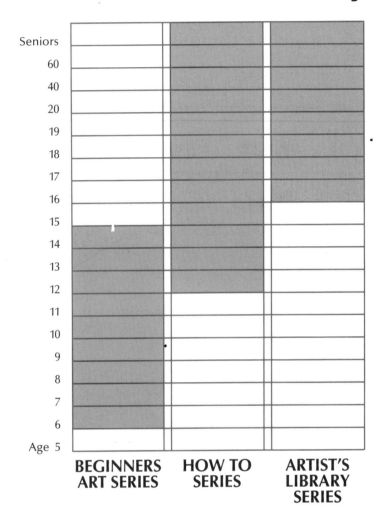

| | BEGINNERS ART SERIES | HOW TO SERIES | ARTIST'S LIBRARY SERIES |

Walter Foster Publishing offers something for everybody! Whether you're a child or an adult, a beginner or an advanced artist, a hobbyist or a professional, we have art books to fit your needs.

Three distinct parts make up the Walter Foster Instructional Art Book System: the **Beginners Art Series,** the **How To Series,** and the **Artist's Library Series.**

The **Beginners Art Series** is designed for children ages 6 and up. Colorful, stimulating and lots of fun, the books in this series teach children the basics of art and art theory while helping them to develop strong tactile and visual skills.

The **How To Series** offers teenage and adult artists at *all* skill levels—from beginning through advanced—first-rate instruction. This extensive series includes more than 100 titles covering every imaginable medium, technique, style and subject.

The **Artist's Library Series** was created expressly for intermediate and advanced artists who wish to expand their creativity, overcome technical obstacles, and explore new media. Each book in this highly praised series is written by a well-known artist uniquely qualified to guide the reader to a new level of expertise.

PAPER ART FUN

ACKNOWLEDGEMENT

The authors, Carolyn Davis and Charlene Brown, would like to thank all of the following for their patience and support: Sally Black, Sally Marshall Corngold, Pat Brown and our friends at Marian Bergeson Elementary and of course, the wonderful staff at Walter Foster Publishing.

INTRODUCTION

Paper art is lots of fun. It also helps develop you visual and tactile skills. You may find it necessary to be very organized to make some of these projects.

We will show you many ways to use paper to make fun art projects. You will learn how tearing or cutting various types of paper can make wonderful designs for pictures and greeting cards. We will also make puppets, papier-mâché projects and even a castle!

These projects make nice gifts, challenging school projects or you can just do them for fun. You can copy our examples or use your imagination to make your own paper art designs.

GLOSSARY

ARRANGE—To place the various parts of your subject in a certain order when planning your project. It is helpful to arrange all the parts before you actually glue or attach them together to make sure the parts are proportional and that the project looks the way you want it to.

CYLINDER—A roll, a ring, or a round object. In this book you will make cylinders out of strips of paper by gluing the ends together.

DIORAMA—A three-dimensional scene that is looked at through a window-like opening, showing a setting with a foreground, a middleground and a background.

MASK—Something that hides or disguises the face. A mask can be funny, scary, or anything you want.

MOBILE—Abstract sculpture or art (as in paper) that hangs in such a manner as to add motion to the art.

OVERLAP—One piece of paper laying over another piece of paper, changing the appearance or color of the paper underneath.

PAPIER-MÂCHÉ—An art form or sculpture molded from strips and pieces of paper and glue.

SLIT—A narrow cut or opening. In this book, we make slits where two pieces of paper attach.

THREE-DIMENSIONAL—Having the characteristics of height, width and depth. A square drawn on a piece of paper is flat, or two-dimensional, and a real cardboard box has depth, which is three-dimensional.

CONTENTS

MATERIALS

POSTER BOARD

SCISSORS

RULER

The ruler is used for measuring and drawing straight lines.

PENCILS

POSTER PAINT

PAINT BRUSH

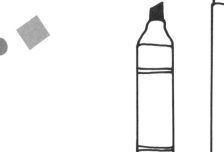

FELT TIP PENS

Felt tip pens come in many bright colors. They can have fine tips or very wide tips, and water base or permanent ink. They are also called marking pens or art markers. You can buy them one at a time or in packages.

GLITTER PAINT

MATERIALS

PAPER

You might need construction paper, poster board, drawing paper and tissue paper. Construction paper comes in bright, bold colors and is a good weight (thickness) for many of the projects. Poster board is stiffer and is needed for certain projects. Tissue paper is very thin and comes in many bright colors. All are easily found in art supply stores.

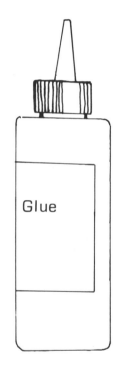

Glue

THINNED WHITE GLUE

We used white glue thinned with water for many of the projects. Mix the glue and water in a bowl and apply it with a paint brush. You may have to experiment to find the best consistency for your project. Here are some mixing suggestions: For papier-mâché, use one part water to three parts white glue. To paint over tissue paper, use one part glue to two parts water.

When painting over construction paper, or when applying a coat of glue to make the surface shiny, use straight white glue—no water.

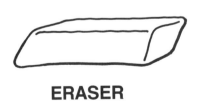

ERASER

1.

PICTURES AND CARDS

Paper art can be lots of fun. By tearing or cutting various shapes out of different types of paper and then gluing, you can make wonderful designs for pictures or greeting cards.

In this chapter we will show you ways to use colorful paper to make a variety of pictures, projects and cards.

You can copy our examples or use your imagination to make your own designs. Paper art is wonderful, colorful fun!

TEAR TISSUE ART

1. Select some bright colors of tissue paper. Tear the paper into fun shapes. We made a bouquet of flowers with our shapes.

2. Arrange the tissue paper shapes on a sheet of white paper. Paint over the pieces of tissue with thinned white glue. Be sure to brush lightly or your tissue might tear (see materials page).

3. See how the shapes overlap and change color. Be careful as the tissue colors can run together.

4. Keep adding tissue pieces until you have created colorful flowers.

10.

11.

CUT AND GLUE

1. Select some bright colors of construction paper. Cut the paper into fun shapes. We made a cat with our shapes.
2. Arrange the shapes on a sheet of white paper. Glue the shapes on the paper.
3. See how the shapes overlap.
4. Keep adding pieces of paper until you have made a colorful cat. (We made the yellow stripes with torn tissue paper.) If you like, you can frame your picture.

12.

13.

VALENTINE CARD

1. Select some bright colors of construction paper. Cut the paper into valentine shapes.
2. Fold a sheet of construction paper in half, like a book.
3. Arrange the shapes (except the hearts) on a small square of white paper, then glue down.
4. Glue the white paper to the front of the folded construction paper.
5. Cut small strips of paper and glue the ends together to make small, round cylinders. Hold the ends together until the glue dries.

6. Glue one side of each cylinder to a heart and the other side to a stem. This makes the hearts stand out from the card.
7. You can use these directions to make other greeting cards. Use your imagination to create your own designs.

15.

BIRTHDAY CARD

1. Select some bright colors of tissue paper. Cut and tear the paper into fun shapes. We made a birthday cake with our shapes.
2. Fold a sheet of construction paper in half, like a book.
3. Arrange your tissue paper shapes on a small square of white paper.
4. When you have the tissue shapes arranged the way you want, paint over them with thinned white glue. Be sure to brush lightly as the tissue might tear (see materials page).
5. See how the shapes overlap and change color. Be careful as the tissue colors can run together.
6. Add more tissue pieces until you have made a colorful cake.
7. Glue the white paper to the front of the folded construction paper.

16.

8. After the glue has dried, you can decorate your card with glitter paint, ribbon, or anything you want.

CHRISTMAS CARD

1. Select some festive colors of tissue paper. Cut the paper into fun shapes. We made a Christmas tree with our shapes.
2. Fold a sheet of construction paper in half, like a book.
3. Arrange the tissue paper shapes on a small square of white paper. Paint over the shapes with thinned white glue. Be sure to brush lightly or the tissue might tear (see materials page).
4. See how the shapes overlap and change color. Be careful as the tissue colors can run together.
5. After the glue has dried, glue the white paper to the front of the folded construction paper. Now you can decorate the tree with glitter paint, ribbons, bows or anything you want.

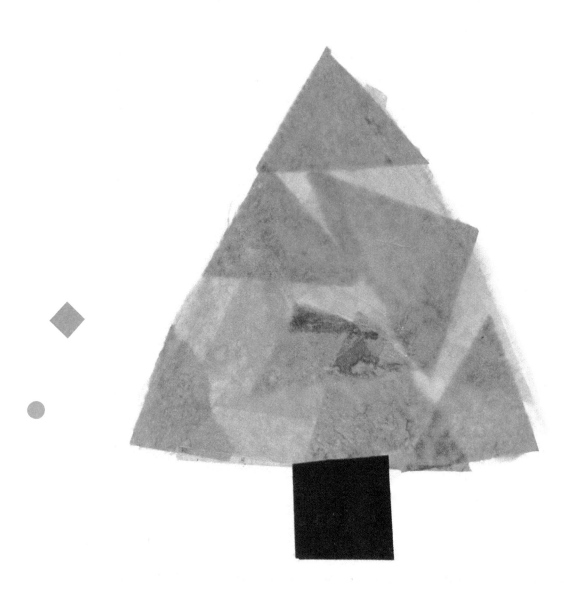

18.

6. We used a hole punch to cut "bulbs" out of aluminum foil, then glued them on the tree.

It's fun to make personalized Christmas cards!

19.

20.

2.

PUPPETS

Puppets are lots of fun to make and to play with. In this chapter we will show you ways to make several different types of puppets. These hand puppets and string puppets will seem to come to life when you use your imagination.

Get ready to entertain your friends with these colorful puppets!

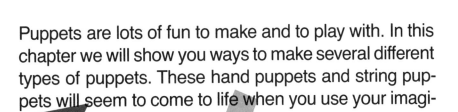

POPSICLE PUPPETS

These puppets can be used behind a table, a countertop or a bed. You can also use them with the puppet theatre on page 58. We made a queen puppet and a king puppet. You can copy our characters, or use your imagination to create your own.

1. Draw your characters on a piece of poster board with pencil. Ink the pencil lines you want to keep, then erase the pencil lines when the ink is dry. (You can also cut characters out of a magazine and glue them on a piece of poster board.)

2. Cut the different parts of the costumes out of tissue paper.
3. Arrange the tissue pieces on your characters, then paint over them with thinned white glue (see materials page).
4. After the glue has dried, you can draw in details or decorate your puppet any way you want.
5. Cut the puppets out.
6. Glue a popsicle stick to the back of each puppet to use as a handle.

Now you can play with your puppets!

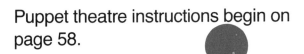
Puppet theatre instructions begin on page 58.

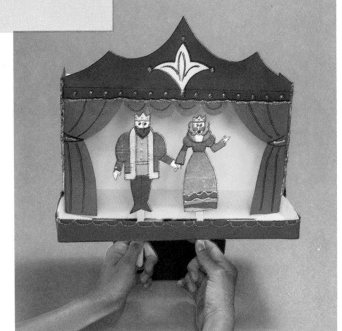

23.

FINGER PUPPET

You can use this puppet with the puppet theatre on page 58. Or, if you prefer, you can just use the puppet on your fingers.

1. Draw your character on a piece of construction paper with pencil. (Your character should not be any larger than your hand.) Ink over the pencil lines you want to keep, then erase the pencil lines when the ink is dry. If you prefer, you can cut characters out of magazines, then glue them to a piece of poster board.
2. Cut the parts of the costume out of construction paper.

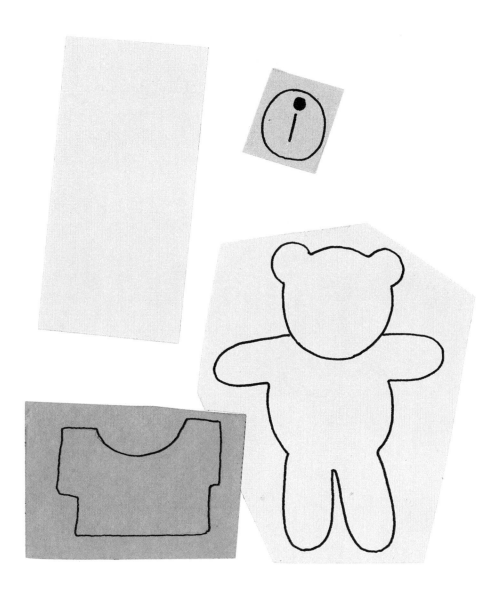

3. Glue the parts of the costume on your character.
4. After the glue is dry, you can draw in details such as the eyes, the nose and the mouth. Now cut your character out.
5. Cut a small strip of construction paper and glue the ends together to make a cylinder (like a ring) for your finger. Hold the ends of the ring together until the glue dries.
6. Glue the cylinder to the back of the puppet.
7. Bend the arms and legs forward as shown.

Now you are ready to entertain your friends!

BAG PUPPET

This magic dragon hand puppet was made out of a lunch bag and pieces of colorful construction paper. You can copy our example, or use your imagination to make your own.

1. Draw the shapes shown on construction paper with pencil, then cut out. (The dotted lines show you where to fold the paper.)

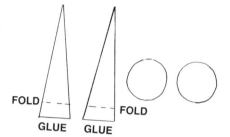

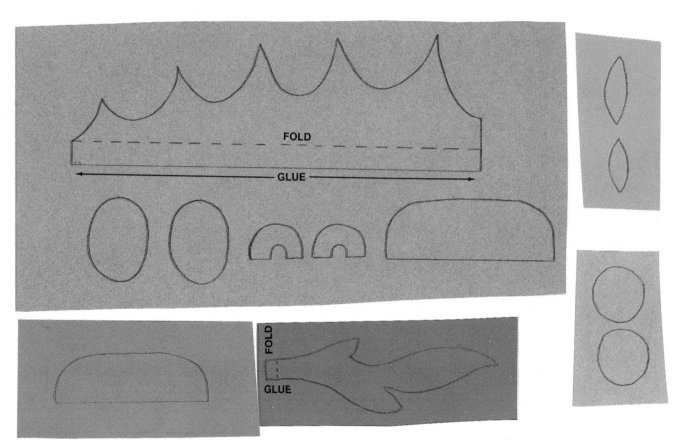

2. Glue the shapes on your bag, as shown. Make sure you do not glue down the flap that allows the bag to move like a mouth.

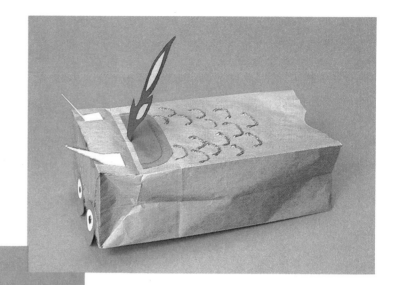

3. If you like, you can use felt tip pens and glitter paint to decorate your magic dragon.

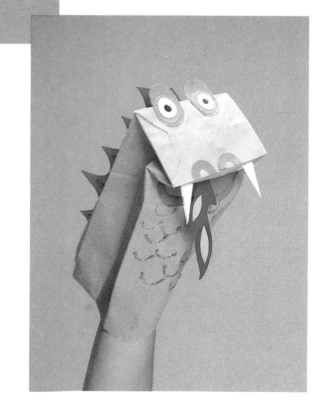

FOLDED HAND PUPPET

This hand puppet was made of colorful construction paper. Use your imagination to create your own character, or follow our example to make a cuckoo bird.

1. Choose a piece of construction paper fifteen inches long and ten and one half inches wide. Fold the paper into three equal parts so the folded paper is three and one half inches wide and fifteen inches long, as shown.

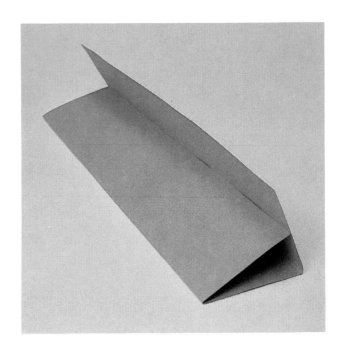

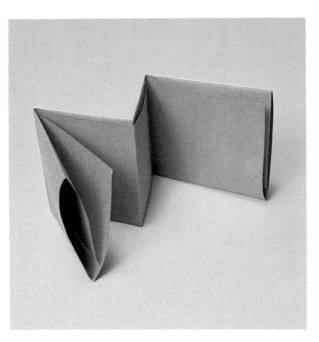

2. Fold the paper in half, then fold the ends back so that the open ends extend about one inch beyond the center fold (see example).

3. Draw the eyes, the tongue, the beak and the feathers on construction paper with pencil, then cut out. The dotted lines show you where to fold the paper.
4. Curl the feathers by wrapping the paper around your finger or a pencil.

5. Fold the ends of the feathers on the dotted lines, then glue on the folded paper.

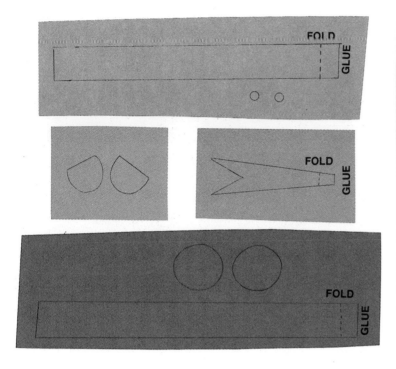

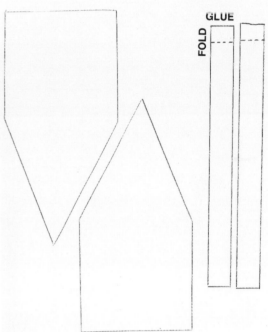

6. Glue the rest of the parts on the folded piece of paper.
7. If you like, you can add things like button eyes, more feathers, or glitter to the top of the head.

Look at this crazy cuckoo bird!

⭐ STRING PUPPET

This puppet was put together with paper fasteners, then strung with string and controlled with sticks, as shown.

1. Draw the parts of your puppet on colorful construction paper with pencil, then cut out. We made a clown with our parts.
2. Glue the head, the body and the hat on one piece of poster board.
3. Glue the hands, the arms, and the sleeve trim on another piece of poster board.
4. Glue the legs, the feet and the pants trim on another piece of poster board.
5. Cut the poster board around the construction paper parts.

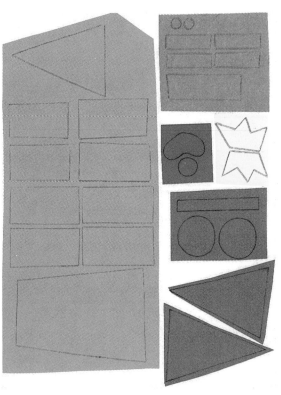

6. Punch holes at the top of the hat, on each hand, and at the elbows, shoulders, hips, knees and feet. Use paper fasteners (called "brads") where shown to attach the parts of the clown together.
7. Put string through the remaining holes and gently, but securely, tie the string.

30.

8. Tie the other ends of the string to two sticks, as shown, or you can tie the string to your fingers if you prefer (you may need a friend to help you do this).

Now your clown is ready to dance for your friends!

31.

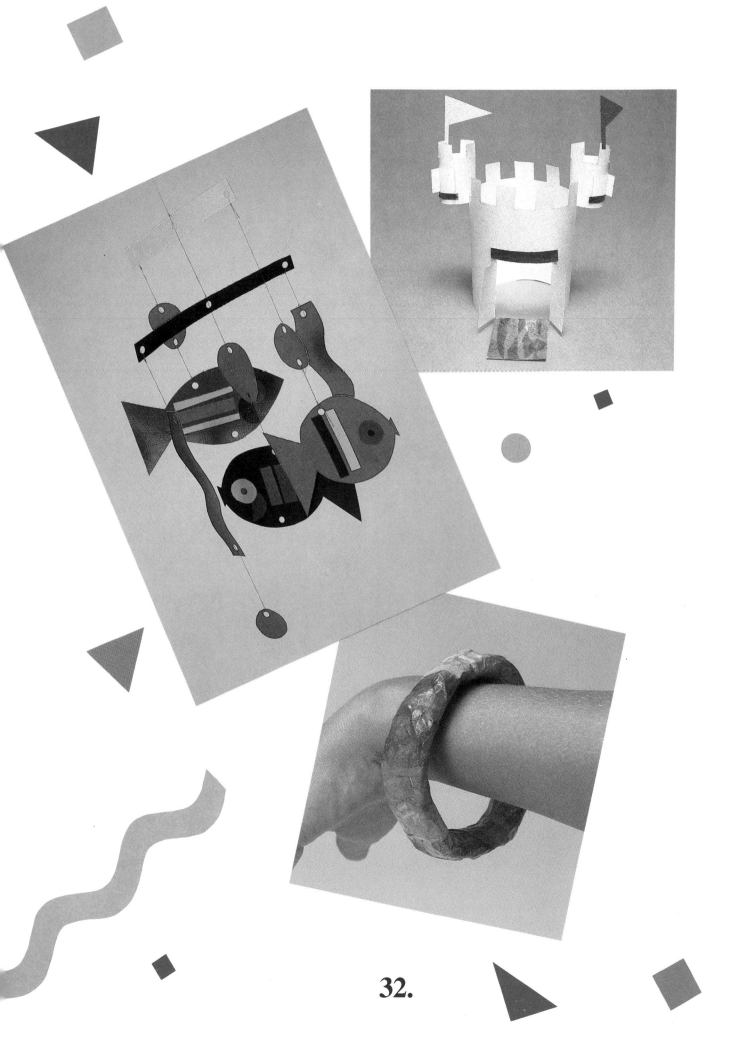

3.

PLACES AND THINGS

In this chapter we will learn how to make fun and colorful three-dimensional projects. We will make a castle, a mobile, and a beautiful bracelet.

These projects are easy to make and lots of fun too! Use your imagination to make them your own creations.

MOBILE

Mobiles are lots of fun and very decorative. You can make a mobile out of any subject. We made a flying aquarium!

1. Draw the parts of your mobile on colorful construction paper with pencil, then cut out.

2. Glue the pieces of your mobile to poster board.
3. Paint over the paper with white glue. Let dry. This makes the pieces shiny.
4. Cut the parts of your mobile out of the poster board.
5. Punch holes at the top of each fish, each bubble and each leaf. (Use a hole punch, not scissors, to do this.)

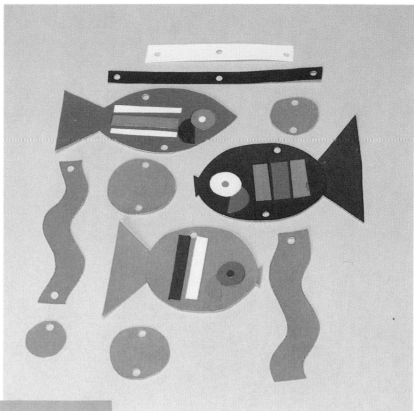

6. Put string through the holes and gently, but securely tie the string.
7. Attach the ends of each piece of string to the ends of a piece of poster board, as shown.
8. Tie a string to the middle of each piece of poster board, leaving some space between each one. This piece of string is for hanging your mobile. (You may prefer to tie your mobile pieces to a wire clothes hanger.)
9. If your mobile does not hang properly, try tying the pieces in a different way to balance it.

BRACELET

These papier-mâché bracelets are easy to make and fun to wear.

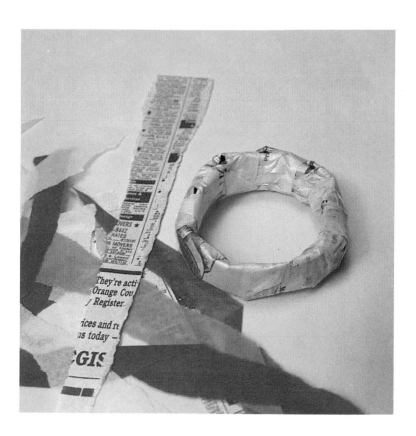

1. Roll some newspaper into a ring (bracelet size), as shown. Use masking tape to hold it.
2. Cut strips of newspaper and dip into thinned white glue (see materials page).
3. Wrap the strips of paper, one at a time, around the newspaper ring until the bracelet is as wide as you want.
4. Let it dry completely. This may take one whole day.
5. Wrap strips of colored tissue around the bracelet until you can't see the newspaper. Paint the strips of tissue with thinned white glue (see materials page).
6. If you like, you can draw or paint designs on the bracelet with a felt tip pen or brush.

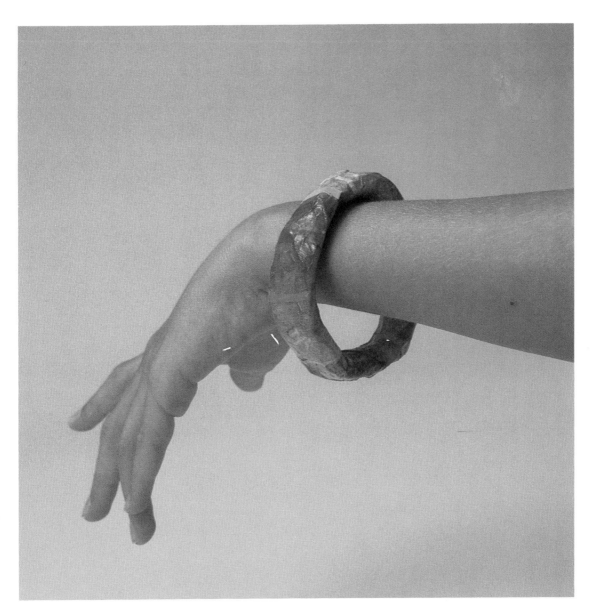

Make different colored bracelets for different outfits!

CASTLE

This is where our queen and king puppets from page 22 live. This castle was made of construction paper and poster board. Use your imagination to make your castle your own design.

1. Draw the castle parts on construction paper with pencil, as shown, then cut out.

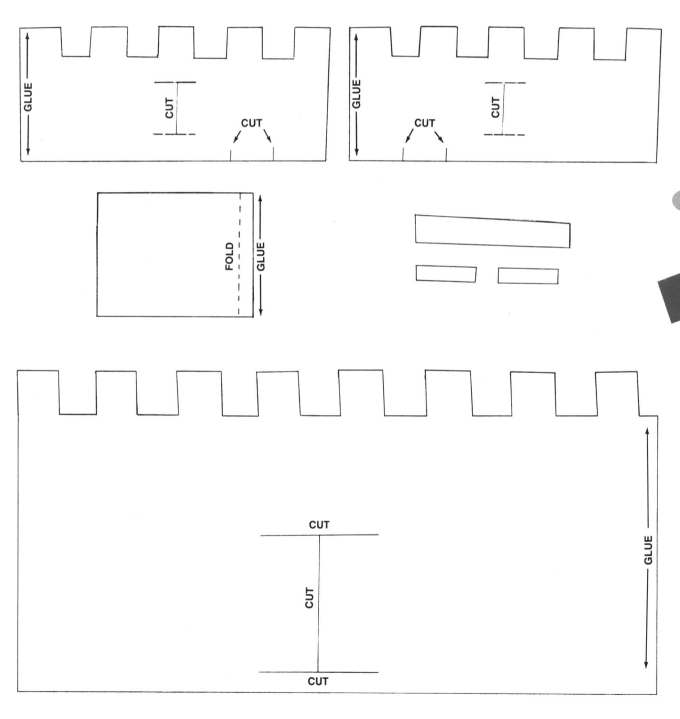

2. Glue the sides of the towers together. Hold the sides together until the glue dries.
3. Glue the sides of the castle together. Hold the sides together until the glue dries.
4. Cut the details out of construction paper. We made shutters, a flag and a drawbridge.

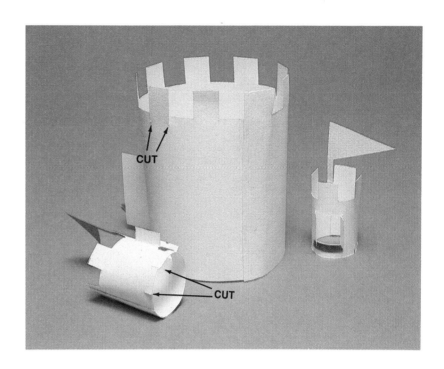

5. Glue these parts to your castle.
6. Make small slits on the bottom of the towers, as shown, then slide them onto the sides of the castle.

This makes a great school project!

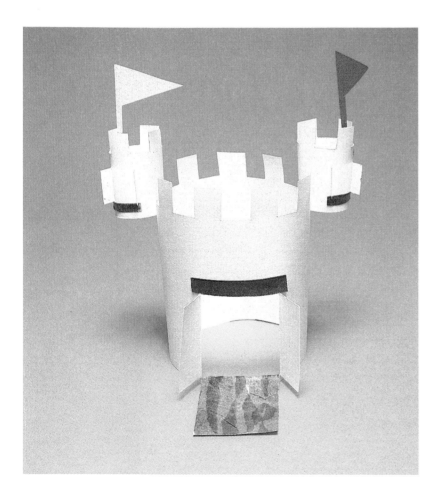

39.

ANIMALS

In this chapter we are going to make a variety of animals using various paper techniques. We will make a mask, a flying bird, and a papier-mâché dinosaur.

These projects are perfect for gifts, school assignments, or just to play with. You can follow our examples or create your own real and imaginary animals using our easy instructions.

PUPPY PENCIL HOLDER

You will need a small, clean can or container with one side open (like an orange juice can) to make this fun pencil holder.

1. Glue a piece of colorful construction paper around your container. Hold the construction paper in place until the glue dries.
2. Draw the puppy shapes on construction paper with pencil.
3. Cut the shapes out.

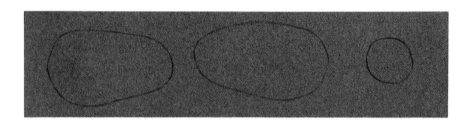

4. Glue the front feet to the container. Hold the paper in place until the glue dries.
5. Glue the back feet to the container. Hold the paper in place until the glue dries.
6. Glue the eyes and the nose to the puppy's face. Draw in details with felt tip pens.
7. Glue the face to the container. Hold the face in place until the glue dries. (We glued the face at an angle to make it stick out from the container.)
8. Glue the ears to the sides of the head. Hold the ears in place until the glue dries.

What a fun gift for your mom or dad!

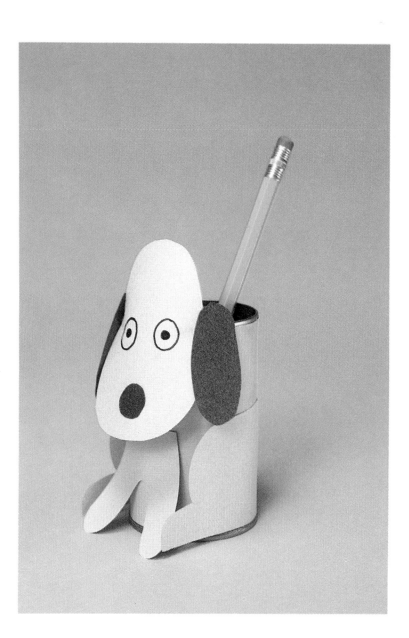

UNICORN MASK

You might want to make a mask for play acting or for Halloween. You can copy our example or use your imagination to create your own mask.

1. Draw the shapes on construction paper with pencil, as shown, then cut out.

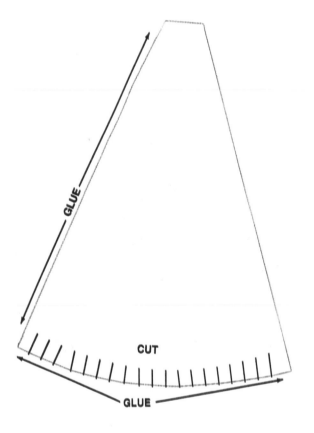

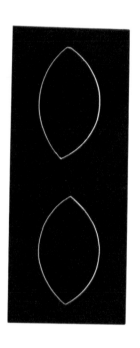

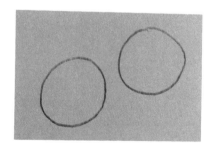

44.

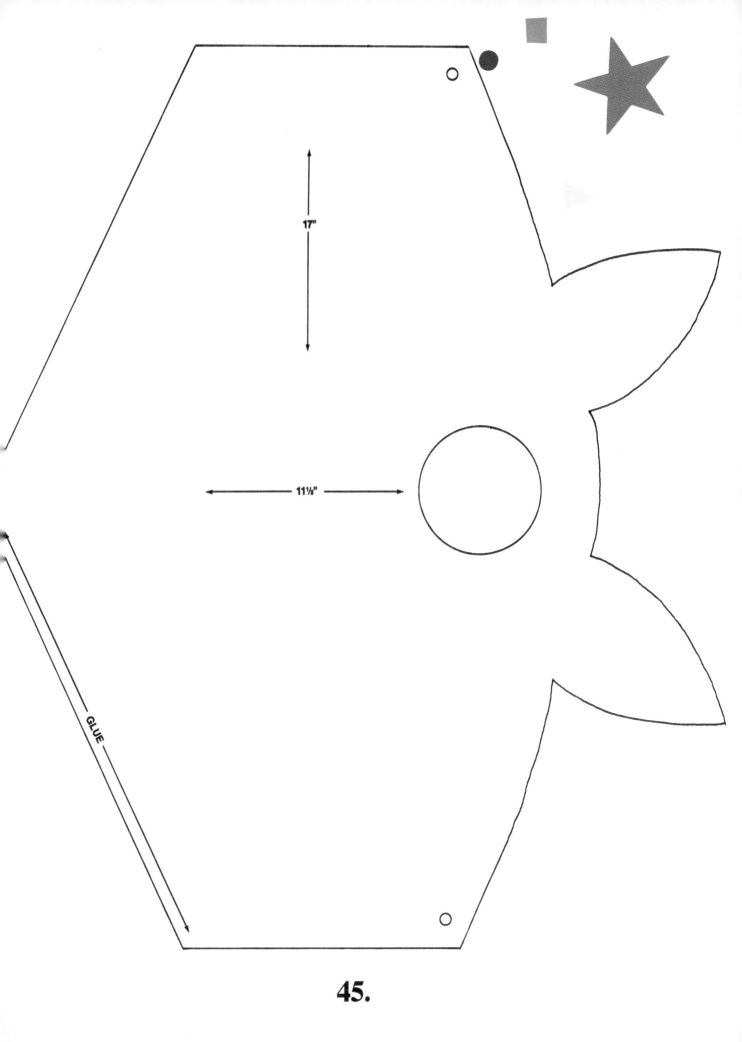

17"

11½"

GLUE

45.

2. Cut slits on the bottom of the horn piece, as shown.
3. Glue the sides of the horn together where shown to make a cone shape. Hold the sides together until the glue dries. Fold the bottom of the horn, along the slits, as shown.
4. Glue the sides of the mask together where shown to form a cone shape. Hold the sides together until the glue dries.
5. Place the horn inside the hole in the head; put the glue where shown. Hold the horn in place until the glue dries.
6. Glue the eyes and the mane on the mask, then cut holes in the eyes so you can see. Be careful pushing the scissors through the paper when you make the holes (you might want to ask an adult to help).
7. Curl the mane by wrapping the paper strips around a pencil or your finger.
8. If you like, you can decorate the horn with glitter paint or felt tip pens.
9. Punch holes into the sides of the mask, then attach some string or ribbon. Now you can wear the mask!

Can you think of other fun masks to make?

47.

FLYING BIRD

This "flying bird" was made of white construction paper and string.

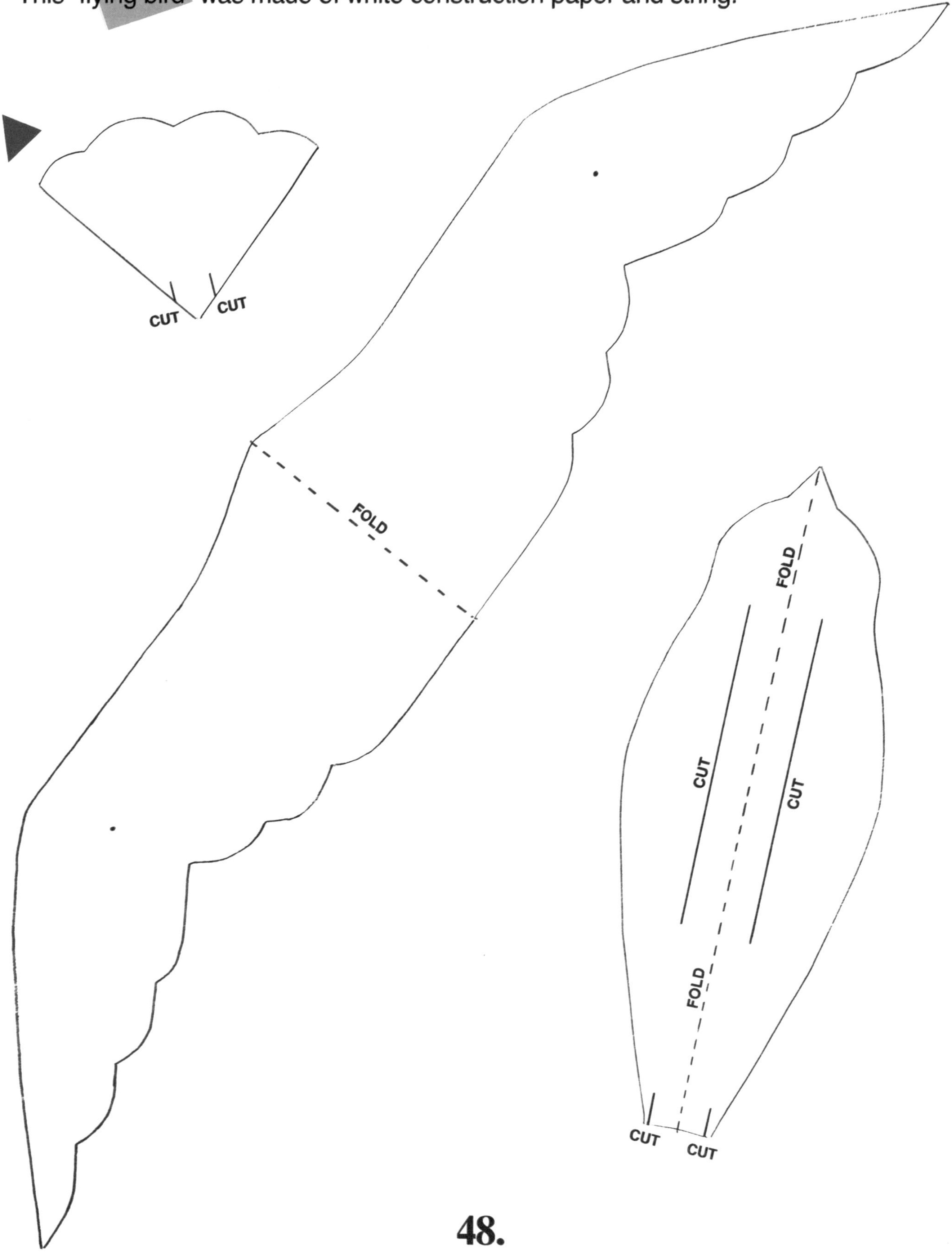

CUT   CUT

FOLD

CUT

CUT

FOLD

FOLD

CUT   CUT

48.

1. Draw the shapes on construction paper with pencil, then cut out. Cut slits where shown.
2. Fold the body and the wings in half, as shown.
3. Attach the tail to the body of the bird by sliding the parts together at the slits.
4. Gently push the wings through both of the slits in the bird's back.
5. Draw or glue paper eyes, wing feathers and a beak on your bird.
6. Punch holes into the wing and tail. Attach string to the bird as shown.

See how your bird flies!

ROCKING HORSE

1. Draw the shape of the horse on two pieces of construction paper, then cut them out at the same time so they are exactly the same.
2. Glue short pieces of thin yarn on the neck of one of the horses to make a mane.
3. Glue some yarn on the rump to make a tail.
4. Glue the two horse bodies together with the glued part of the yarn on the inside. Do not glue the horses' legs together.
5. If you like, you can use glitter paint, ribbon or construction paper to decorate the horse, or to make him a saddle and reins.

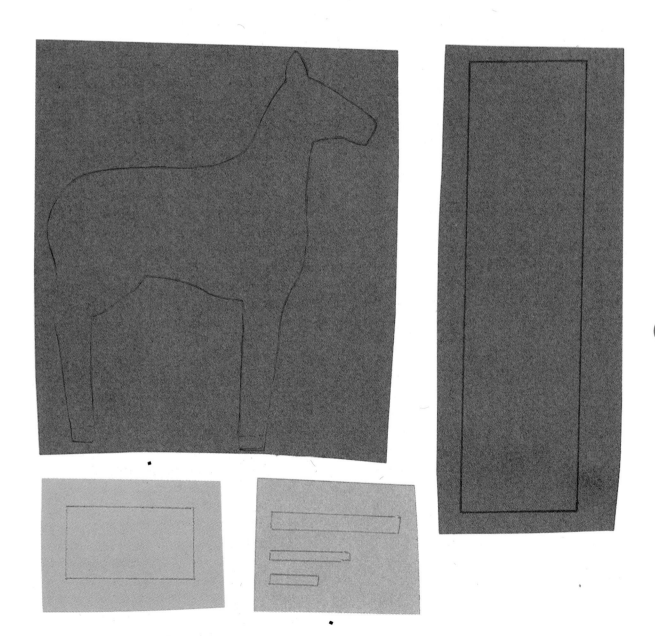

6. Cut out paper rockers for the horse.

7. Bend the rockers gently and glue to the feet of the horse.

Giddyap!

51.

DINOSAUR

This scary green dinosaur was made of papier-mâché and strips of tissue paper, then decorated with construction paper and felt tip pens. You can copy our example or make any animal you want by following the same steps.

1. Shape the dinosaur's body out of crunched newspaper. Tape the newspaper tightly together with masking tape.
2. Shape the head and neck out of rolled newspaper, as shown.
3. Tape the head and neck of the dinosaur to the body.
4. Shape a tail out of rolled newspaper and tape to the body.

5. Roll up small cylinders for the legs and tape these to the body.
6. One by one, dip strips of newspaper into thinned white glue and place on the dinosaur's body to shape and smooth the dinosaur. Do this until you create the shape you want. You can make several layers of paper strips.
7. Apply strips of colored tissue paper with thinned white glue until the newspaper is covered. Be very careful with the tissue paper as it can be difficult to take off if it sticks to the wrong place.

8. Allow the dinosaur to dry completely. This may take a whole day.

9. Glue construction paper spikes to the back of the dinosaur.

10. Use paint, felt tip pens or construction paper to add the details of the face and scales.

Papier-mâché is fun!

5.

MORE PROJECTS

The three-dimensional projects in this chapter are a little more challenging than the subjects in the previous chapters. These projects can be used for school, gifts, or to entertain your family and friends.

Remember, the examples we demonstrate are just some of the projects you can make. Use your imagination to make your own creations.

WINDMILL

This windmill was little more challenging than the previous projects because you have to use your ruler to measure the pieces. You can copy our example or use the same steps to make a skyscraper, a lighthouse, or anything you want.

1. With light pencil, draw the mill and the sails of the wheel on construction paper. Use a ruler to measure the widths of the tops and bottoms of the panels to make sure they are all the same. Leave an extra one quarter inch flap on one of the ends for gluing.
2. Draw details with felt tip pen.
3. Glue the construction paper parts onto a piece of poster board.
4. Cut the parts out of the poster board, then fold the mill as shown in the example.

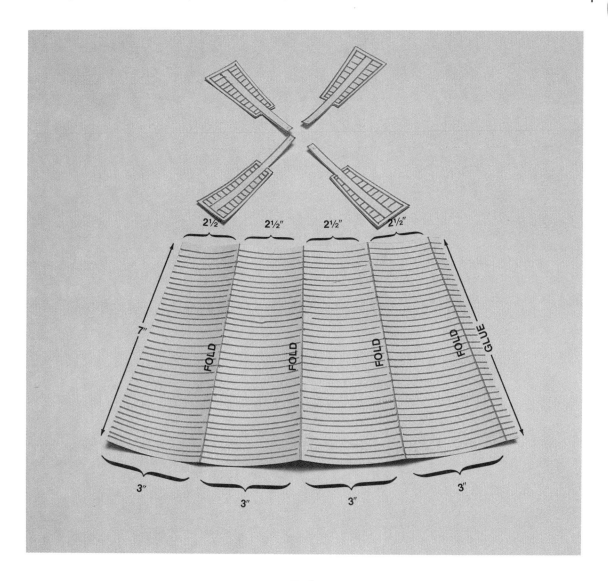

5. Glue the sides of the mill together. Hold the sides together until the glue dries.
6. Attach the sails of the wheel to the front of the mill with a paper fastener, as shown.

Now your windmill is ready for a wind storm!

PUPPET THEATRE

Here is a fun place for your popsicle stick puppets and your finger puppets to perform. You can copy our example or decorate your puppet theatre any way you like.

You will need a shoe box for this project. Ask permission if it doesn't belong to you.

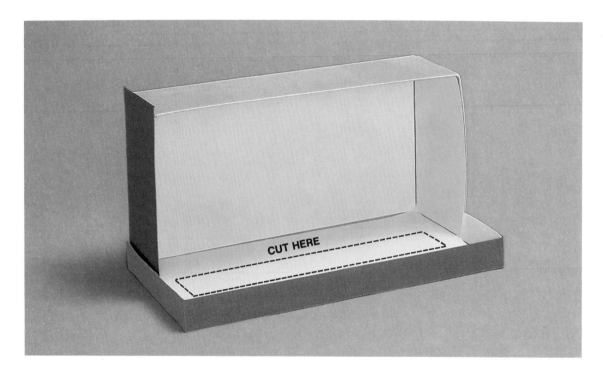

1. Glue the lid to the side of the box for the floor of theatre.
2. Cover the inside and the outside of the box with bright colored construction paper.
3. Cut a long rectangle in the front of the floor of the stage. This is where your puppets come to life.
4. Cut curtains out of construction paper and glue to the box as shown.
5. If you like you can decorate your theatre with felt tip pens, construction paper, glitter paint or anything you want. You might want to look in books or magazines for ideas.

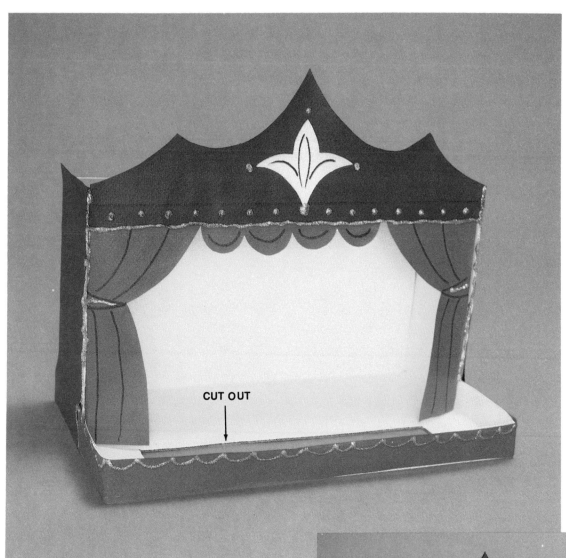

Now you're ready for a puppet show!

Popsicle puppet instructions begin on page 22.

59.

DINOSAUR DIORAMA

You can make a diorama of any subject you want. We made ours prehistoric. Copy our example or use your own idea.

You will need a shoe box to make this project. Ask permission if it doesn't belong to you.

1. Cover the box with construction paper.
2. Find some books or magazines that have pictures of dinosaurs and their environment (such as trees, bushes, rocks . . .). Decide what kinds of dinosaurs and landscape you want to use in your diorama (or use your own subject).
3. With light pencil, draw the dinosaurs, bushes, trees and other parts of the landscape on different colors of construction paper. Try to make them look realistic.
4. Add details with felt tip pens. Cut the parts out of construction paper.
5. Glue the first layer (the sky and the bushes) to the back of the box. These are the things that are furthest away.

61.

6. Glue the next layer (more bushes) in front of the first layer by folding the edges of the construction paper (as shown), and gluing them to the sides of the box.

GLUE

GLUE

FOLD

FOLD

7. Now glue the next layer (trees, bushes and a dinosaur) by folding the edges of the construction paper and gluing them to the bottom of the box, in front of the second layer.

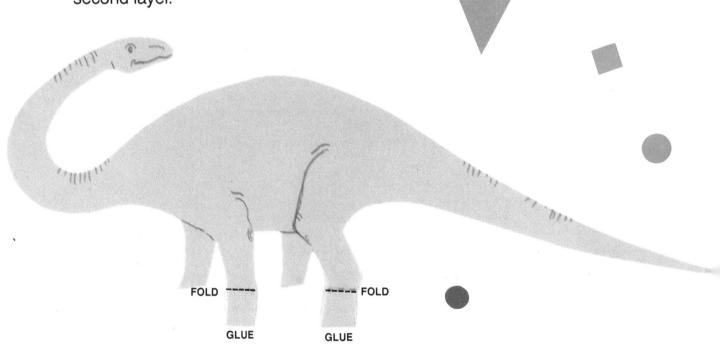

FOLD ----- ----- FOLD

GLUE GLUE

62.

8. Glue the rest of the parts to the bottom and sides of the box. Place the parts in front of one another to create a three-dimensional effect. You can follow our example or do it the way you think looks best.

Making dioramas is fun!

Beginners Art Series

Walter Foster's **Beginners Art Series** is a great way to introduce children to the wonderful world of art. Designed for ages 6 and up, this popular new series helps children develop strong tactile and visual skills while having lots of fun! Each book explores a different medium and features exciting "hands-on" projects with simple step-by-step instructions.

- **Drawing Fun** begins with basic shapes children know, and progresses to instruction on shading, shadows, and perspective.
- **Color Fun** teaches the fundamentals of color theory: color identification, color mixing, and color schemes.
- **Clay Fun** demonstrates clay sculpting techniques, and acquaints children with several different types of clay.
- **Comic Strip Fun** teaches children how to draw facial expressions, body movements and character interaction.

- **Poster Fun** introduces basic design and lettering skills, then uses these techniques to create posters, greeting cards, and games.
- **Paper Art Fun** shows how to create a variety of paper art objects from everyday materials like construction paper and paper bags.
- **Cartoon Fun** teaches beginning artists how to use simple shapes to create cartoon characters.
- **Painting Fun** teaches the fundamentals of painting with watercolor, acrylic, oil, and poster paints.
- **Felt Tip Fun** demonstrates the use of a variety of felt tip and marker pens through projects ranging from two-dimensional art to a puppet and a diorama.
- **Colored Pencil Fun** offers a series of two- and three-dimensional art projects which help children learn fundamentals such as shading, color blending, and basic drawing.

Age	5	6	7	8	9	10	11	12	13	14
Drawing Fun										
Color Fun										
Clay Fun										
Comic Strip Fun										
Poster Fun										
Paper Art Fun										
Cartoon Fun										
Painting Fun										
Felt Tip Fun										
Colored Pencil Fun